JOAN OF ARC: THE PEASANT GIRL WHO LED THE FRENCH ARMY

BIOGRAPHY OF FAMOUS PEOPLE
CHILDREN'S BIOGRAPHY BOOKS

Speedy Publishing LLC

40 E. Main St. #1156

Newark, DE 19711

www.speedypublishing.com

Copyright 2017

All Rights reserved. No part of this book may be reproduced or used in any way or form or by any means whether electronic or mechanical, this means that you cannot record or photocopy any material ideas or tips that are provided in this book.

In this book, we're going to talk about the courageous life of Joan of Arc. So, let's get right to it!

WHO WAS JOAN OF ARC?

Joan of Arc was an amazing young woman. At a young age, she had visions that told her she would help to save the country of France from the English. She believed that these visions were messages from God and when she got old enough she decided to follow God's destiny for her.

EARLY LIFE

Joan of Arc was born in the small town of Domremy, France in the year 1412. Jacques, her father, had a farm and he also held a position as a town official. Like many young girls her age, Joan did chores on the farm and her mother Isabelle taught her to sew. Joan was very religious. She loved her faith and believed strongly in the angels and saints.

BASILIQUE DE DOMREMY

INSIDE OF BASILIQUE DE DOMREMY

VISIONS FROM GOD

When Joan was about twelve or thirteen years of age, she began to hear heavenly voices. The first time it happened she was in her family's garden. She heard voices coming from the right side, which was the direction of the church. The voices also had a bright light with them and sometimes they would come to her when the church bells were ringing.

At first, she saw a vision of St. Michael, the Archangel, and heard his voice. When she saw him, many other heavenly angels were with him. He told her that with God's help and the help of St. Catherine and St. Margaret that she would lead French soldiers against the armies of the English. After the English were driven out of the country, she was to make sure that the French king would be crowned at the city of Rheims.

ST. MICHAEL, THE ARCHANGEL

Joan felt strongly that the visions and voices she was experiencing were from God, his angels, and his saints. They told her specifically what she was to do although she had no training as a warrior or military leader. Joan continued to have these visions. She wept when the angels and saints left her presence. She would have preferred to be taken into heaven with the angels, but she had an important destiny to fulfill first.

When she turned sixteen years old, Joan felt that she was ready to move forward with what God, the angels, and saints were asking her to do.

JOURNEY TO MEET WITH KING CHARLES VII

Joan was a farm girl from a peasant family. She had no special training in the military. She had no army to lead. Her voices told her to gain an audience with King Charles. She began this journey by going first to the closest town.

STATUE OF JOAN OF ARC IN THE BASILICA OF SACRE COEUR IN PARIS

KING CHARLES

There, she approached Count Baudricourt, who was the garrison commander, to ask him if he would help her in her quest to speak with the king directly. Even though Joan couldn't read or write, she was very articulate as well as persistent. Count Baudricourt didn't take her seriously and laughed at her request.

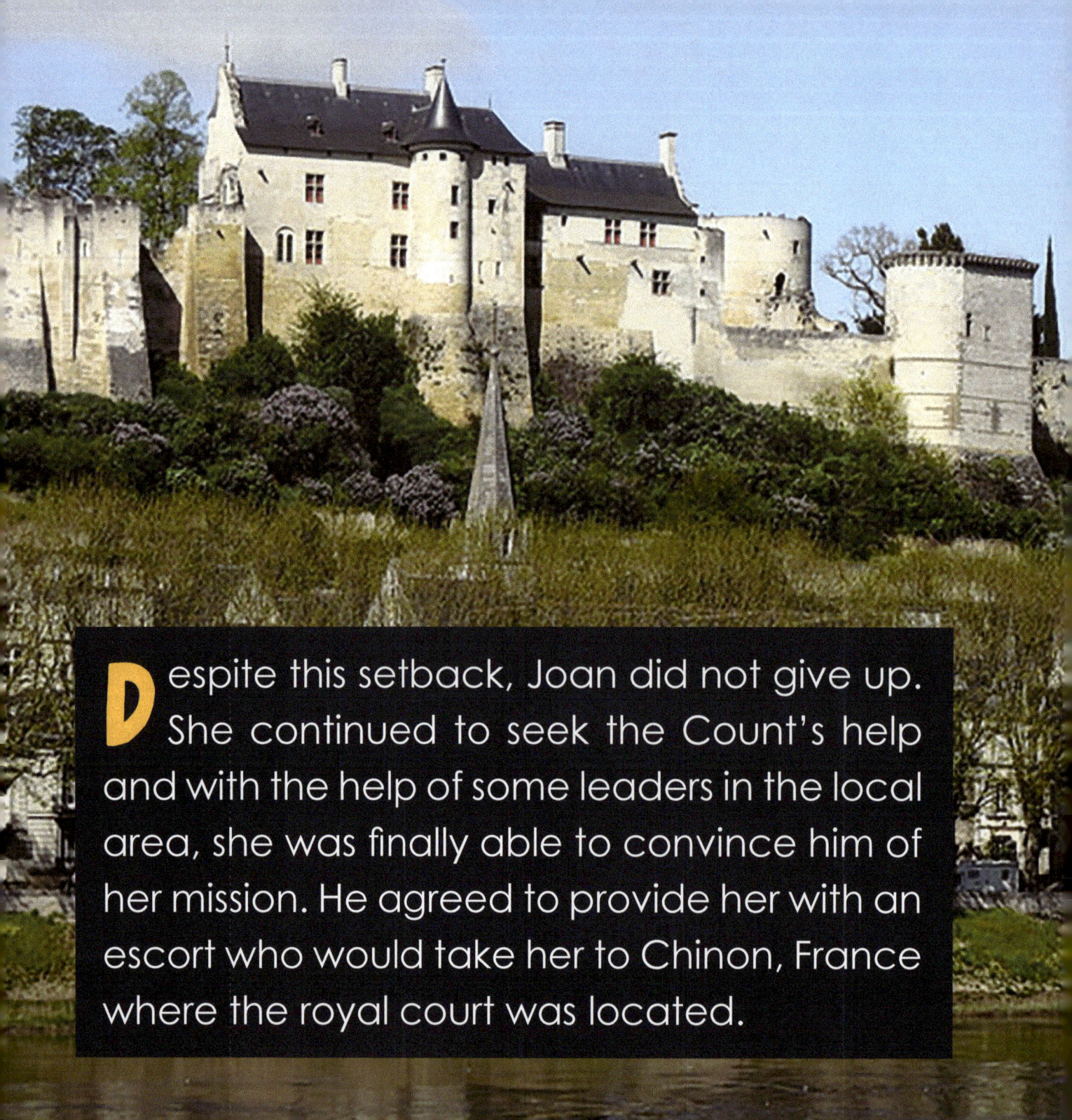

Despite this setback, Joan did not give up. She continued to seek the Count's help and with the help of some leaders in the local area, she was finally able to convince him of her mission. He agreed to provide her with an escort who would take her to Chinon, France where the royal court was located.

STATUE OF JOAN OF ARC

Joan cut her hair short and dressed in men's clothes so that she could travel the 11-day journey to Chinon.

MEETING KING CHARLES VII

Joan's voices had told her that when she met with the king, he would be given a sign that what she was experiencing was real. She trusted her voices and went forward to have a private audience with the king.

JOAN AT THE ROYAL COURT

At the beginning, the king was very suspicious of Joan's intentions. He had heard a great deal about her already and wasn't sure if she was sane or crazy. When Joan arrived at the royal court, the king hid amongst the other members of his court. Joan had never seen him before.

In those days there were no photographs and she wouldn't have had access to a portrait of him. Despite that, she walked right up to him in the midst of the others and addressed him as her king.

CHARLES VII WEARING THE CROWN

The king was not yet convinced that she was genuine and holy. However, something changed during the course of their meeting. No one knows precisely what happened in her meeting with the king. There is no historical transcript of what they said to each other. Legend has it that she told him something he had said in a prayer that no one else knew about.

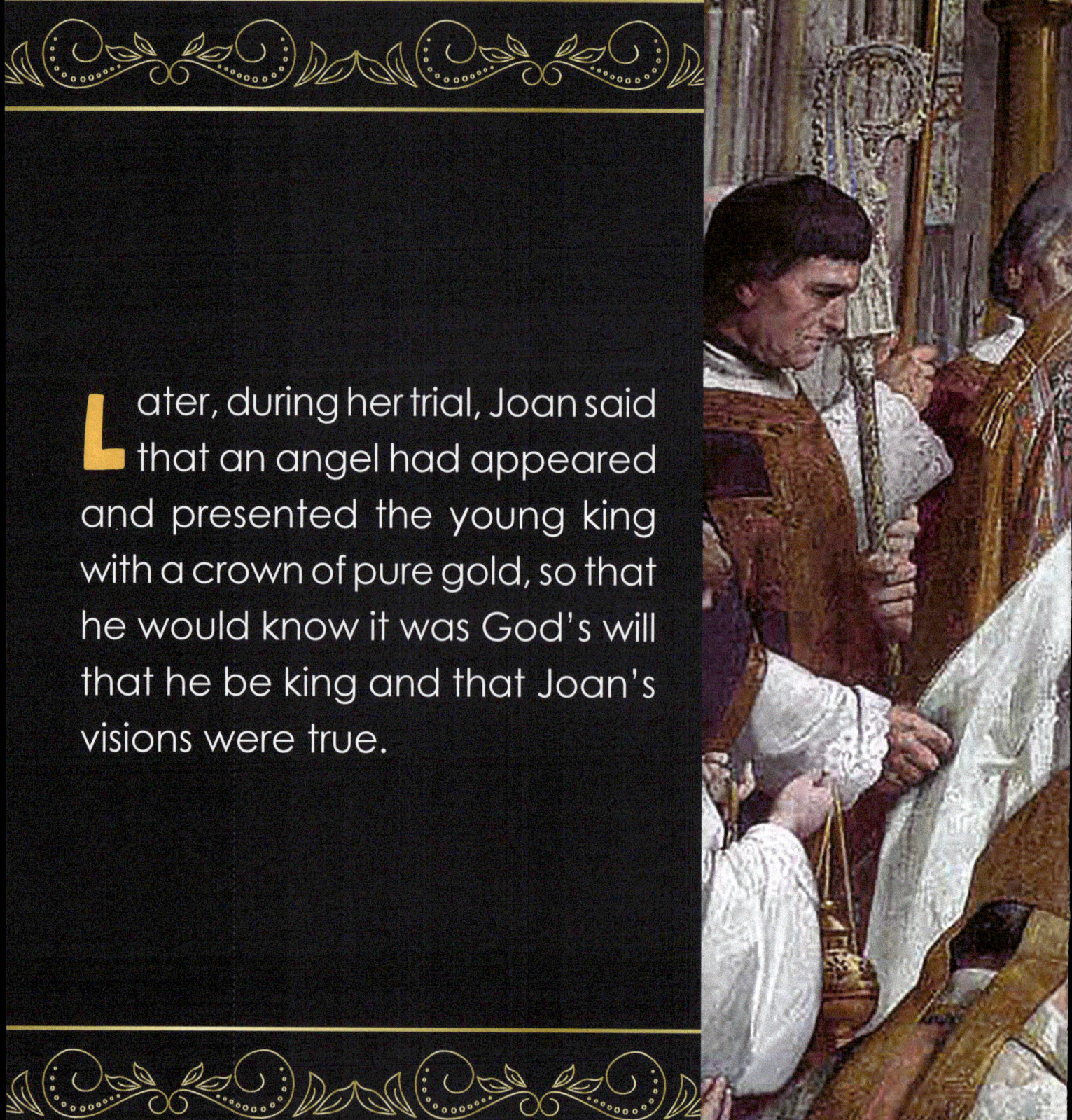

Later, during her trial, Joan said that an angel had appeared and presented the young king with a crown of pure gold, so that he would know it was God's will that he be king and that Joan's visions were true.

THE CORONATION OF KING CHARLES

MONUMENT TO JEANNE D'ARC IN ORLEANS, FRANCE

After discussing the situation with his advisors, the king decided that he would take the risk of having Joan move forward with her plan. He had much to gain if she were successful and little to lose if she was not. He let her accompany a group of soldiers and military supplies to Orleans, France, which was under siege by English soldiers.

While she was waiting for the king's arrival, she practiced to become a warrior and proficient at riding a horse. When the king gave his signal, she was ready to begin the battle.

SIEGE OF ORLEANS

As Joan traveled to Orleans, news about her was being reported from town to town. The people of France began to believe that she had been truly sent by God and that this young woman, who was just a teenager, had the ability to spare them from the English forces. When Joan arrived at Orleans, she was met with cheers and hopeful celebrations.

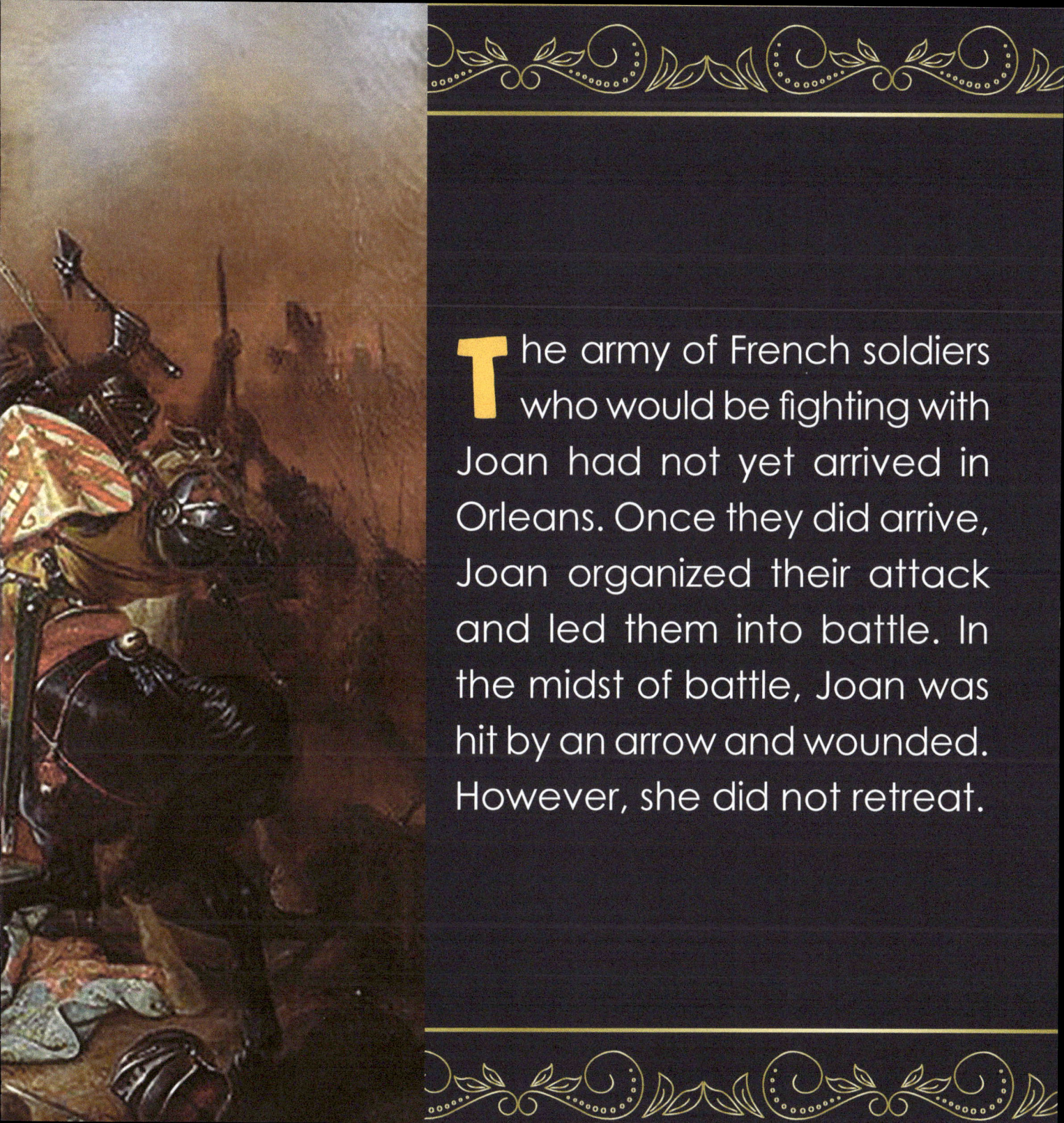

The army of French soldiers who would be fighting with Joan had not yet arrived in Orleans. Once they did arrive, Joan organized their attack and led them into battle. In the midst of battle, Joan was hit by an arrow and wounded. However, she did not retreat.

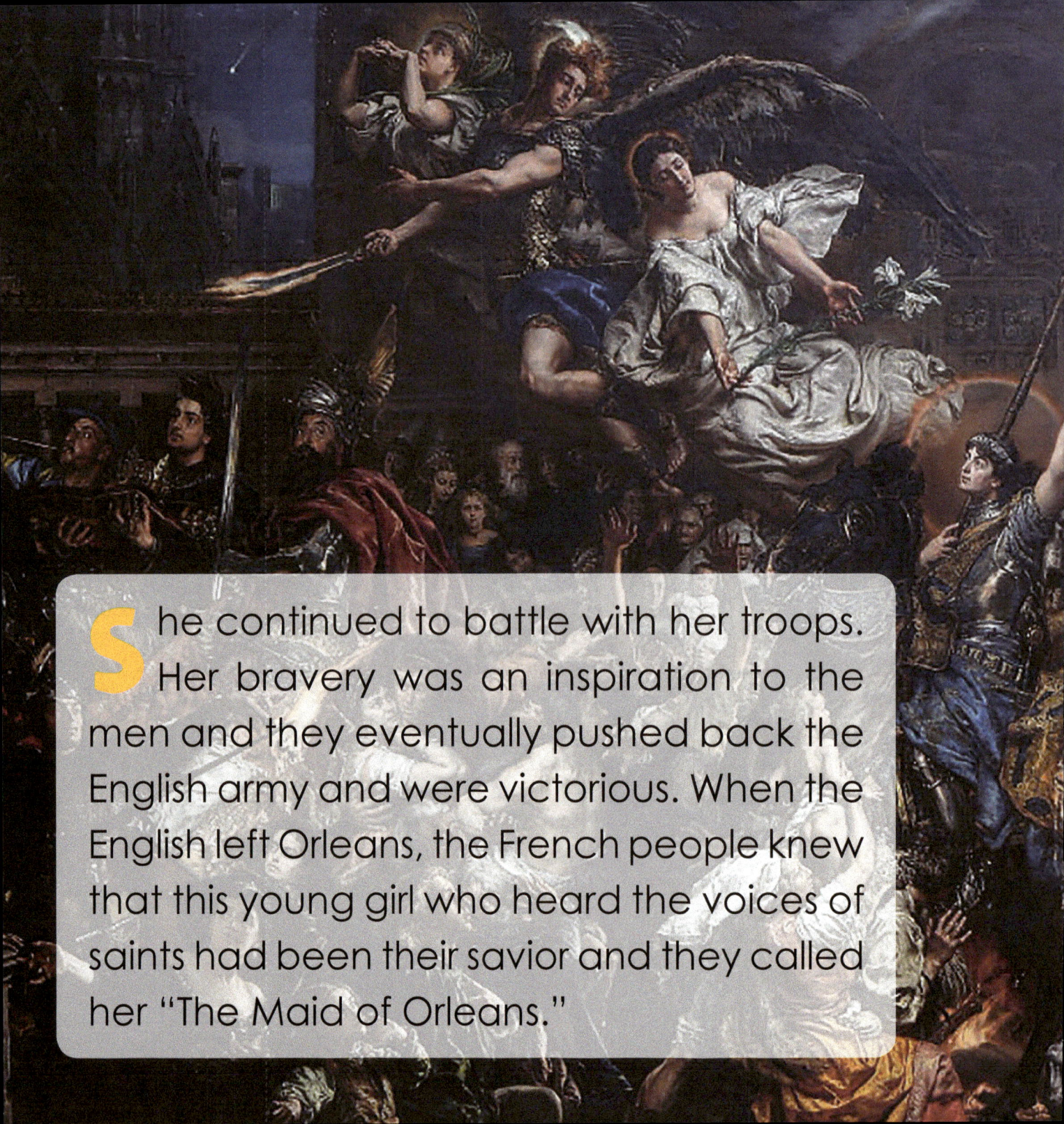

She continued to battle with her troops. Her bravery was an inspiration to the men and they eventually pushed back the English army and were victorious. When the English left Orleans, the French people knew that this young girl who heard the voices of saints had been their savior and they called her "The Maid of Orleans."

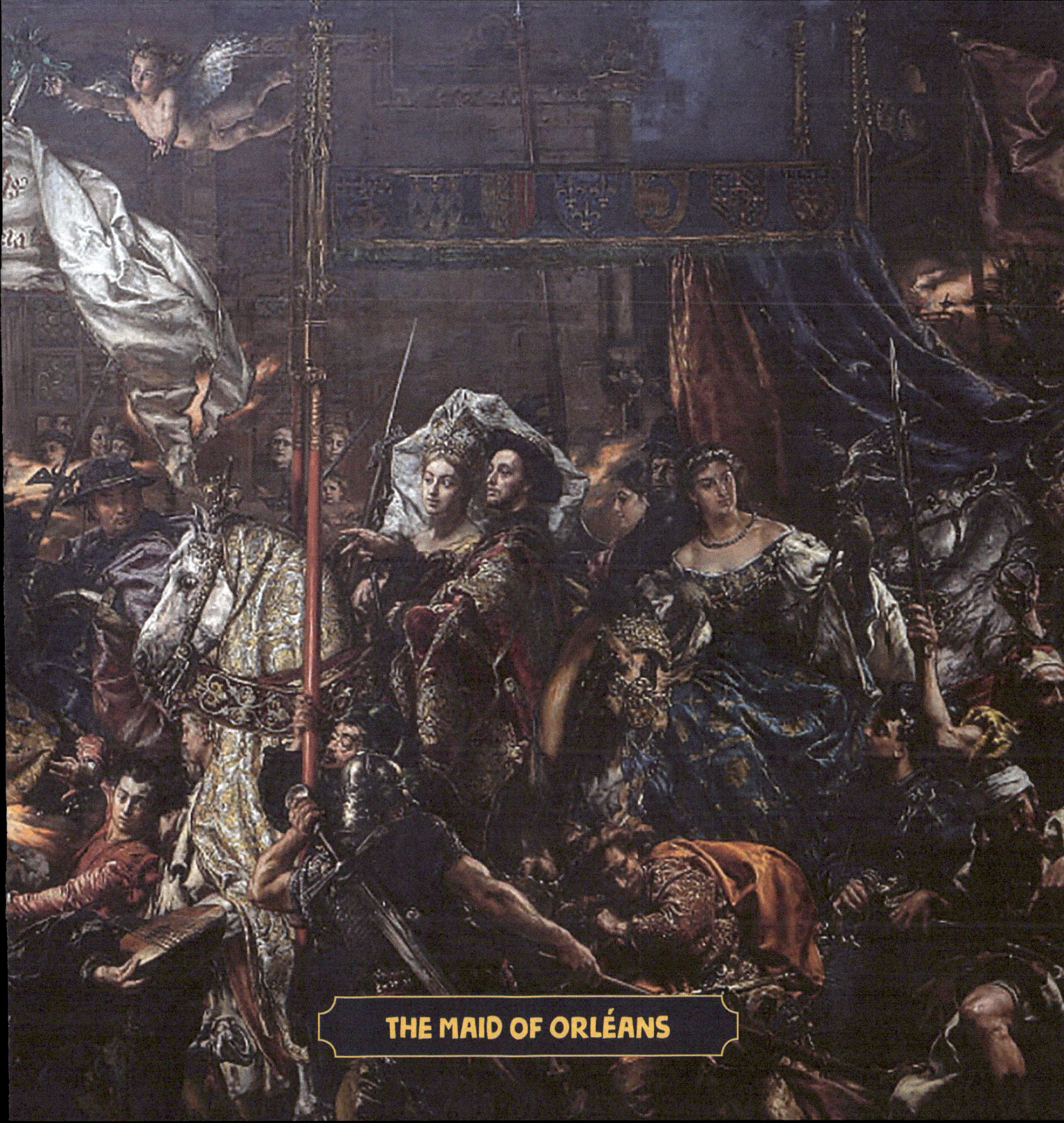

THE MAID OF ORLÉANS

KING CHARLES IS CROWNED

After she and her troops had won the Battle of Orleans, Joan knew that there was more for her to do. Her spiritual visions and voices had told her to escort Charles to Rheims. There he would be officially crowned king. Joan and her soldiers cleared the path to Rheims and as they traveled the countryside her reputation grew and she gained loyal followers.

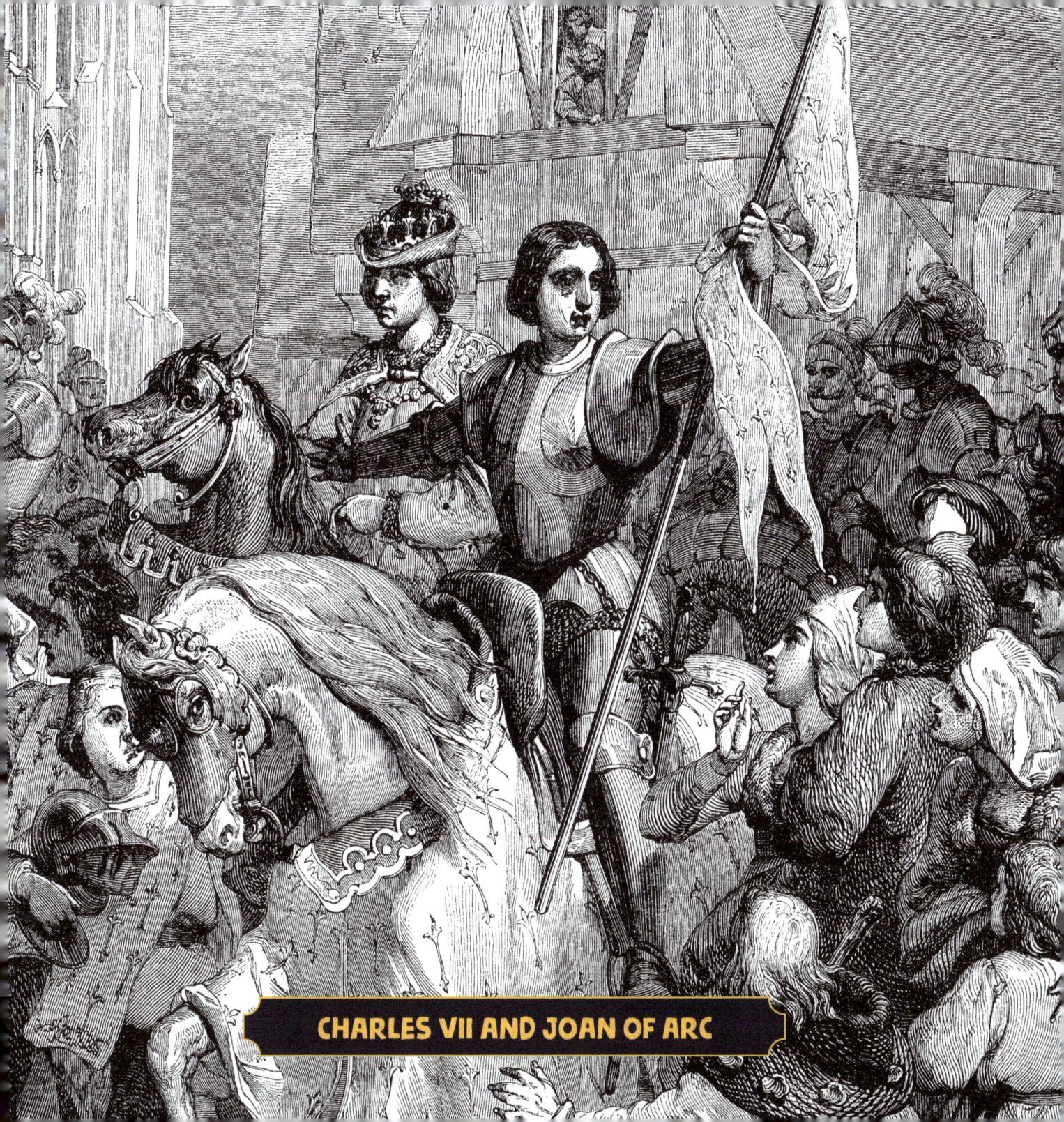
CHARLES VII AND JOAN OF ARC

THE CORONATION AT RHIMS

They soon arrived at the city of Rheims where Charles was officially given the crown and the position as the King of France.

CAPTURED BY THE BURGUNDIANS

The city of Compiegne, France was under siege by the Burgundians. Joan took a small group of soldiers with her and went to fend off the attackers. She and her soldiers were outside the city battling the attackers when the city leaders raised the drawbridge to protect the citizens and keep them safe.

ROYAL CASTLE OF COMPIEGNE, FRANCE

MAIN ENTRANCE WITH DRAWBRIDGE OF THE CASTLE

They didn't realize it, but they had left Joan in a position where she was vulnerable to capture. Joan was taken prisoner and then sold to the English.

TRIAL AND DEATH

The mighty English army and leaders were humiliated by the defeats they had suffered at Joan's hands. Such a girl must be a witch to have commanded these powers. They put Joan on trial to prove that she was a heretic and was practicing witchcraft. After asking her many questions about her religious experiences and questioning her purity, they couldn't find a reason to convict her.

They had to have an excuse to put her to death, so they claimed she had done the work of the devil because she had cut her hair short and worn men's clothes.

When they sentenced her to death, Joan's strength failed and she professed that the voices she had heard weren't real. However, while she was in prison, she claimed that the saints had visited her because they were disappointed that upon penalty of death she had denied that they were real.

JOAN OF ARC CAPTURED BY THE BURGUNDIANS

JOAN OF ARC IN PRISON

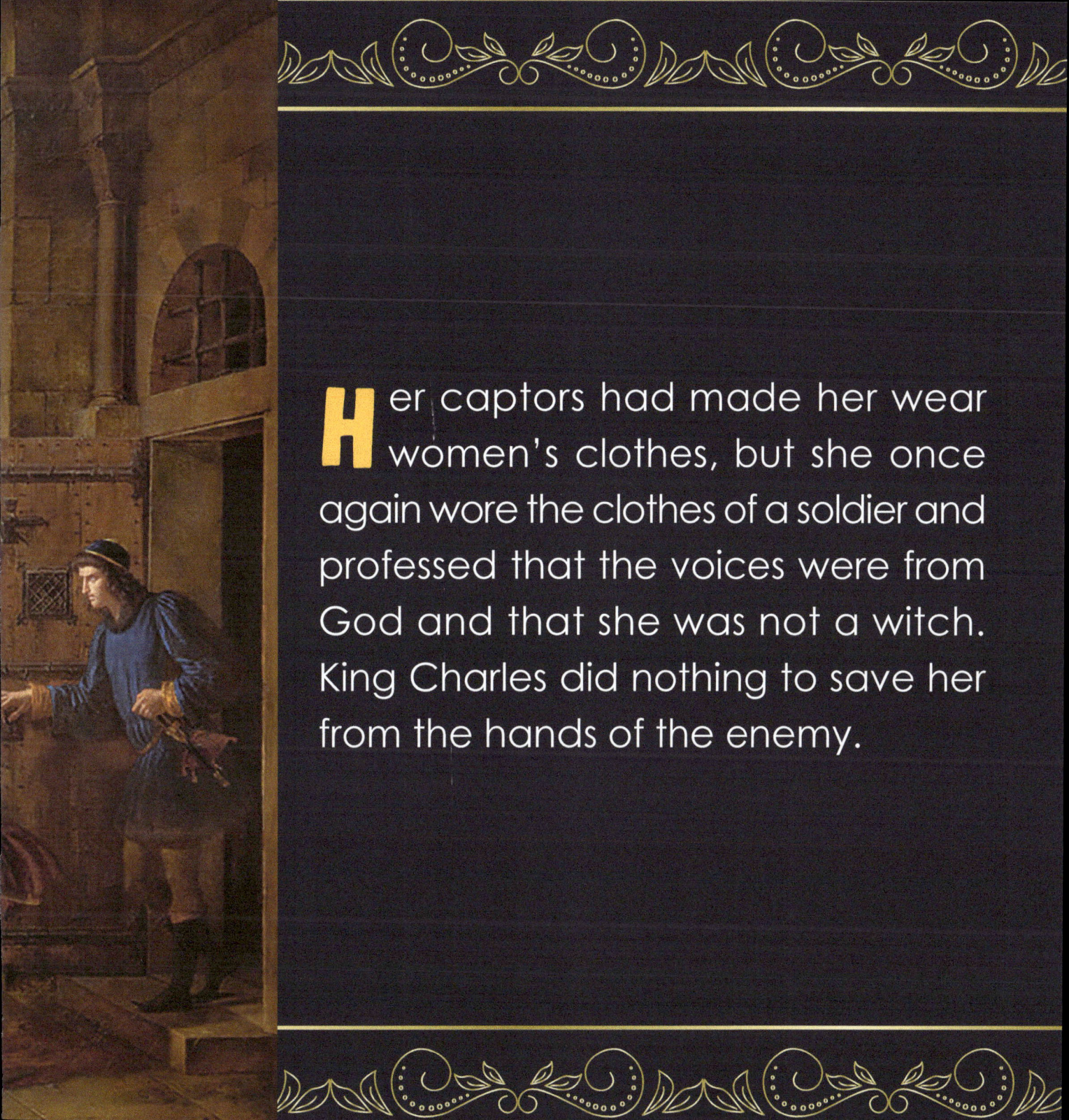

Her captors had made her wear women's clothes, but she once again wore the clothes of a soldier and professed that the voices were from God and that she was not a witch. King Charles did nothing to save her from the hands of the enemy.

The English tied Joan to a stake in the ground and burned her while she was still alive. She asked to be given a cross and one of the English soldiers who was witnessing the tragedy gave her a wooden cross to hold as she died. She was only 19 years of age.

JOAN OF ARC'S DEATH AT THE STAKE

MODERN STATUE OF JOAN OF ARC IN NOTRE-DAME DE PARIS CATHEDRAL INTERIOR, PARIS

Legend says that her heart wouldn't burn and the English had to burn her body three times before it became ashes. In 1920, Joan of Arc was proclaimed a saint by the Roman Catholic Church.

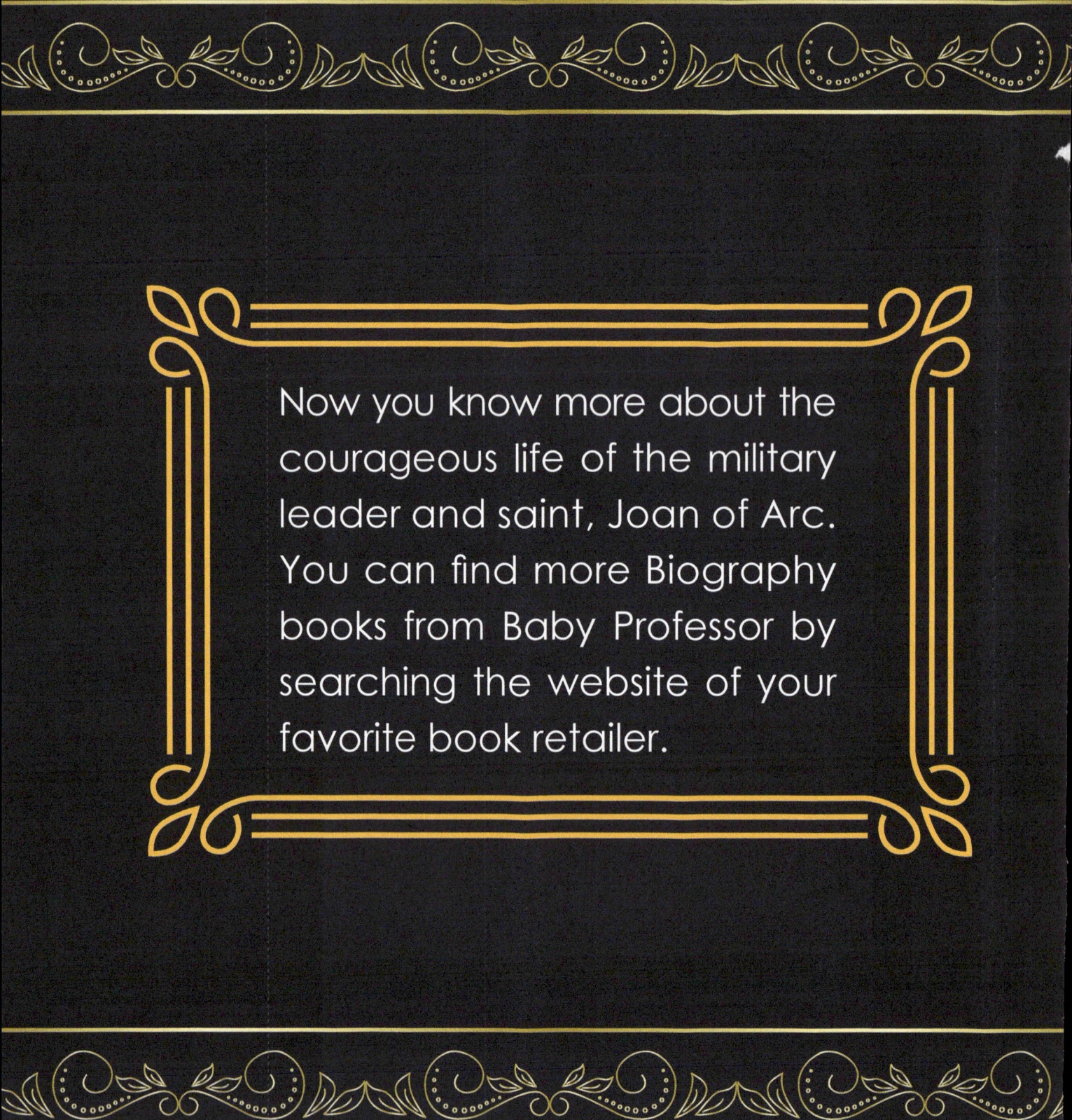

Now you know more about the courageous life of the military leader and saint, Joan of Arc. You can find more Biography books from Baby Professor by searching the website of your favorite book retailer.

Milton Keynes UK
Ingram Content Group UK Ltd.
UKHW050116050924
447642UK00021BA/90